The
Digestive System

Injury, Illness and Health

Carol Ballard

Heinemann Library
Chicago, Illinois

Originated by Ambassador Litho
Printed and bound in Hong Kong, China by South China Printing Company

07 06 05 04 03
10 9 8 7 6 5 4 3 2 1

Library of Congress Cataloging-in-Publication Data
Ballard, Carol
     The digestive system / Carol Ballard.
          v. cm. -- (Body focus)
Includes bibliographic references and index.
Contents: The digestive system -- Chemical digestion -- Nutrition -- Problems with nutrition -- In the mouth -- Teeth -- Esophagus -- Stomach -- Stomach problems -- Small intestine -- Large intestine -- Intestinal problems -- Liver -- More about the liver -- Pancreas -- Diabetes -- Kidney structure -- Kidney function -- Kidney problems -- Bladder and urination.
     ISBN 1-4034-0195-0 -- ISBN 1-4034-0451-8 (pbk.)
     1. Digestive organs--Juvenile literature. 2. Digestion--Juvenile literature. [1. Digestive system.] I. Title. II. Series.
     QP145 .B258 2003
     612.3--dc21
                                                            2002014420

Acknowledgments
The publishers would like to thank the following for permission to reproduce photographs:
p. 9 Gareth Boden; p. 10 Photodisc; p. 14 Getty Images/UHB Trust; p. 16 Corbis; p. 17 Science Photo Library/Mehau Kulyk; p. 20 Science Photo Library/J. C. Revy; p. 23 Science Photo Library/Biophoto Associates; pp. 24, 30, 32, 33 Science Photo Library; p. 26 Science Photo Library/Science Pictures; p. 27 Science Photo Library/David M. Martin; p. 29 Science Photo Library/Professor P. Motta, Dept. of Anatomy, University "La Sapienza"; p. 31 Science Photo Library/Department of Clinical Radiology, Salisbury District Hospital; p. 34 Rex Features; p. 35 Science Photo Library/Saturn Stills; p. 40 Science Photo Library/Richard J. Green; p. 41 Corbis Stock Market/Michael Heron.

Cover photograph of a colored X-ray, showing the inside of the intestines, reproduced with permission of Science Photo Library.

The publishers would like to thank David Wright for his assistance with the preparation of this book.

Every effort has been made to contact copyright holders of any material reproduced in this book. Any omissions will be rectified in subsequent printings if notice is given to the publishers.

Some words are shown in bold, **like this.** You can find out what they mean by looking in the glossary.

CONTENTS

THE DIGESTIVE SYSTEM

Our bodies cannot make use of the food we eat until it is broken down into smaller, **soluble** particles. This breaking-down process is called **digestion,** and the organs that carry it out are called the digestive system. The process happens automatically whenever we eat. Food is broken down, the particles of food are absorbed into the blood, and waste is removed from the body.

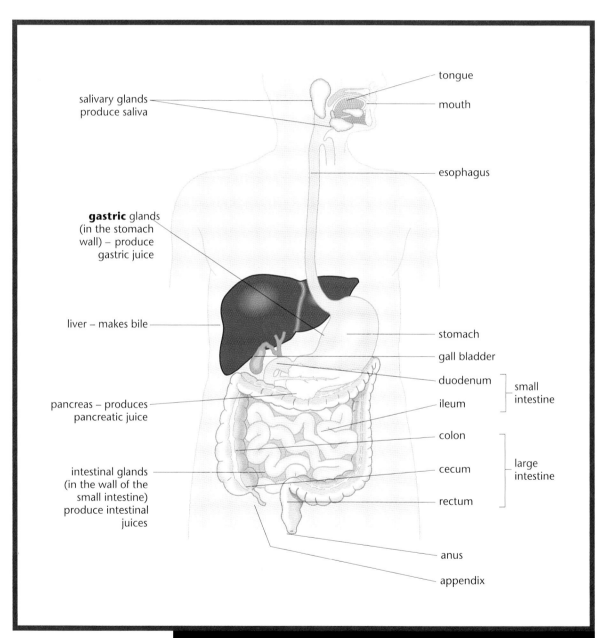

salivary glands produce saliva

tongue

mouth

esophagus

gastric glands (in the stomach wall) – produce gastric juice

liver – makes bile

stomach

gall bladder

duodenum

ileum

small intestine

pancreas – produces pancreatic juice

colon

intestinal glands (in the wall of the small intestine) produce intestinal juices

cecum

rectum

large intestine

anus

appendix

The digestive system processes the food we eat so that our bodies can make use of the chemicals the food contains. This picture shows the main parts of the digestive system and other organs that are involved with the digestive process.

Food gives our bodies the building blocks for growth and repair, the chemicals our bodies need to stay fit and healthy, and energy as well. Eating the right amounts of the right types of food is important—eating too much or too little food can lead to health problems. Not eating a particular food type can also cause problems.

The digestive system is made up of a continuous tube that runs from mouth to **anus**—the alimentary canal—as well as other related organs. Food begins its journey through the alimentary canal as we bite into it with our teeth. The teeth mash the food, and the **saliva** in the mouth begins to digest it. Our sense of smell helps us to identify and taste what we are eating, and alerts us to food that may be harmful. Our tongue contains millions of taste buds that allow us to distinguish many different flavors.

When we swallow, the softened food passes into a pipe called the esophagus. This pipe carries the food down to the stomach, where digestive juices attack the food, breaking it down even more. The food, now a liquid, passes into a long, narrow tube called the small intestine. Here, more juices are added from the small intestine, liver, and **pancreas**. The particles that our body can use are absorbed into the blood and carried to every part of the body. Waste passes into the large intestine, where water is absorbed into the bloodstream and the waste becomes drier and more solid. This solid waste, called **feces,** is stored in the rectum until we use the toilet. Then it leaves the body through the anus.

Although not directly involved in digestion, other organs are important in processing the food we eat. The liver regulates the levels of sugars and other chemicals in the blood. The kidneys clean the blood, filtering out any waste chemicals and excess water. The bladder stores the liquid waste, called urine, until we use the toilet. Then the urine leaves the body through a narrow tube called the urethra.

Physical and chemical digestion

Your food is digested in two main ways:
- Physical digestion happens when food is broken into smaller pieces by your teeth and tongue. Food is also broken down by muscles that push it down the alimentary canal.
- Chemical digestion happens when **enzymes** and other chemicals break down the food at various stages, starting with the saliva in the mouth. This process is made easier because the food has already been broken into smaller pieces by physical digestion.

NUTRITION

The parts of food that our bodies can use are called **nutrients.** Different foods provide different nutrients. To stay healthy, we need to eat a balanced diet—a variety of foods, in the right proportions, providing all the nutrients that we need.

We can divide foods into six main groups:
Bread, pasta, rice, flour, and cereals: These foods contain **carbohydrates,** either as starches or as sugars, that our bodies use for energy. Unrefined carbohydrates, like wholegrain cereals and wholemeal flour, also contain fiber, a substance that helps the digestive system to function properly. Refined carbohydrates, such as white flour and white sugar, contain little or no fiber and are of less value to the body.

Vegetables: These are important sources of **vitamins** and **minerals** needed to maintain general good health. For example, vitamin A is needed for healthy skin and hair, and iron is needed for red blood cells to carry oxygen efficiently. Calcium, found in some leafy vegetables, is important for growth and maintenance of strong, healthy teeth and bones. Vegetables also provide fiber, the cellulose material that plant cell walls are made of. This has no nutritional value, but it is important in helping the digestive system to work efficiently. We are not able to **digest** fiber, so it adds bulk to the **feces** and makes them softer, helping them to pass out of the body more quickly and easily. Lack of fiber in the diet can lead to bowel problems.

Fruits: These are also important sources of vitamins and minerals. Citrus fruits, such as oranges and grapefruits, are rich in vitamin C, a nutrient that helps to boost the **immune system.** Like vegetables, fruits contain fiber and therefore help the digestive system to function efficiently.

Dairy products such as milk, yogurt, butter, and cheese: These are rich in **fats** that we use for energy. One gram of fat will give about nine calories (40 joules) of energy. Dairy products are also good sources of calcium, some vitamins, and **proteins.**

fats, oils, & sweets (use sparingly)

meat, poultry, fish, dry beans, eggs, & nuts group (2–3 servings)

milk, yogurt, & cheese group (2–3 servings)

vegetable group (3–5 servings)

fruit group (2–4 servings)

bread, cereal, rice, & pasta group (6–11 servings)

Today, many doctors suggest that we should try to get most of our energy from starchy foods such as bread, pasta, and rice, and avoid eating a lot of sugar and fat. Think of our daily food intake as a pyramid: eat plenty of the bottom layers, less of the middle layers, and just a little of the top layers!

Foods for energy	Food	Calories
Energy is measured in units called calories (cal). We need to balance the amount of energy we use with the amount of energy we get from our food. Some foods contain more energy than others. This table compares the amount of calories in some different types of food.	Apple, medium	80
	Butter, 1 tablespoon	100
	Cheddar cheese, 1 ounce	115
	Chicken breast, 3 ounces	140
	Chocolate, 1 ounce	145
	Pasta, 1 cup cooked	200
	Salted peanuts, 1 cup	840

Meat, fish, eggs, nuts, and beans: These foods are good sources of proteins, which our bodies need for growing and for repairing damage. Proteins are made from smaller units called **amino acids.** The human body cannot make amino acids, but we can change some amino acids into others. However, there are at least eight amino acids (called essential amino acids) that we cannot make in this way, so we have to obtain them from our food. It is easy to obtain all of them from animal sources, but vegetarians who avoid these sources have to make sure that they eat a wide variety of different protein foods, since few of them contain all the essential amino acids.

Fats and oils: These are found naturally in many foods, and we often add them to foods when serving or cooking. Some meats are very fatty, and cooking oils and dairy products such as butter consist almost entirely of fat. These are good sources of energy and provide important chemicals that the body needs for a variety of purposes. However, a diet high in fatty foods is bad for us, because the body stores excess fat instead of getting rid of it as waste.

Another vital part of a balanced diet is water. About 60–70 percent of a human body is water! Although we can survive for several weeks without food, we can survive only a few days without water.

Malnutrition

Malnutrition occurs when a person's diet has not provided sufficient proteins or energy for a prolonged time. With too little protein and too few calories, people's muscles waste away and their growth is impaired. A diet rich in carbohydrates but lacking in protein leads to a swollen abdomen and wasting muscles. Both types of malnutrition are common in children from areas of the world affected by famine.

CHEMICAL DIGESTION

Digestion is the process of breaking down food into smaller particles that can be used by the body. Different foods are digested in different ways, by different parts of the digestive system. Food is digested physically when we chew it into smaller pieces. As it passes through the digestive system, chemicals digest the food into separate particles.

Enzymes

Enzymes are **proteins** that make chemical reactions happen. They act as catalysts, speeding up the reactions, but they do not get used up themselves. One enzyme can be used over and over again. Each enzyme is specific—it can do only one job.

Digestive enzymes break down large food **molecules** into much smaller units. There is a different type of enzyme for each type of food molecule. Most enzyme names end with "ase," and the name usually gives some clue about what the enzyme does—for example; a protease breaks down proteins.

Proteins

Not all proteins are enzymes. Dietary proteins are found in foods like meats, fish, eggs, and nuts. They are very large molecules, made up of smaller units called **amino acids.** There are about twenty different amino acids in animal proteins. A small protein molecule might contain about 100 amino acid molecules, arranged in their own special order.

Protein digestion

This table shows where different enzymes are produced in the body, what they act on, and what molecules are produced by this action.

Breakdown of proteins into single amino acids begins in the stomach. A protease enzyme breaks protein molecules down into smaller molecules called peptides. The **pancreas**, an organ that lies below the stomach, produces a liquid called pancreatic juice. This juice contains several more proteases and peptidases. It is added to the partly digested food in the small intestine, where its enzymes help to break down the peptides into individual amino acids.

Type of enzyme	Produced by	Action
amylase	salivary glands in mouth, pancreas	starch → maltose → glucose
protease and peptidase	stomach and pancreas	proteins → peptides → amino acids
lipase	pancreas	fats → fatty acids + glycerol

Foods such as breads and cakes are rich in carbohydrates.

Carbohydrates

Carbohydrates are found in foods that contain starch or sugar, such as bread, cereals, and pasta. They are made from a simple sugar called **glucose.** Two molecules of glucose joined together make another sugar, called maltose. Lots of glucose molecules can be joined together to make polysaccharides like **glycogen** or starch.

Carbohydrate digestion

Carbohydrates need to be broken down into single glucose molecules. The digestion of starch begins in the mouth. **Saliva** contains an enzyme called salivary amylase that acts on starch, beginning to break it down into maltose. When the maltose and any remaining starch reach the small intestine, the pancreatic amylase in pancreatic juice finishes breaking them down into molecules of glucose.

Fats

The scientific name for **fats** and oils is lipids. One molecule of fat is made up from three smaller units called **fatty acids,** plus one unit of glycerol. Different fatty acids make up different kinds of fats.

Fat digestion

In the small intestine, **bile** produced by the liver is added to the partly digested food. This liquid contains bile salts that break the fats into small drops. These small drops are then broken down even further by lipase, an enzyme in pancreatic juice. It helps to separate the molecules of fatty acids from the molecules of glycerol.

PROBLEMS WITH NUTRITION

If our diet does not provide all the **nutrients** we need, or if we eat more than we need, we will not be healthy.

Obesity

Obesity is the medical term for being very overweight. Although there can be a variety of reasons for obesity, it is usually the result of eating too much and exercising too little. Being obese can lead to health problems, including heart disease and diabetes.

Body weight

If we take in the same amount of energy as we use, our weight will stay the same. If we take in more energy than we use, our weight will go up, as our bodies store the extra energy as **fats** or **glycogen.** If we take in less energy than we use, our weight will go down, as our bodies use up some of their stores of fats or glycogen. It is important to try to keep a balance between the amount of food we eat and the amount of energy we use. Being very overweight or very underweight is bad for our overall health.

Eating disorders

Two common eating disorders are anorexia nervosa and bulimia. People who suffer from anorexia worry excessively about being overweight, even though they are usually very thin. People suffering from anorexia generally eat very little at meal times or skip meals altogether. They may try to disguise how little they are eating by piling their plate with foods such as salad, which give them very little energy or **protein.** Friends and family may point out to them that they are already thin and need to eat more, but many anorexics are unable to believe them and

Junk food is often very high in fats and **carbohydrates.** It's fine to eat food like this occasionally, but eating it at every meal could lead to health problems.

Using energy

Even when we are sleeping, our bodies use energy to maintain vital processes such as heartbeat, breathing, brain function, and body temperature. The more active we are, the more energy we use up. The amount of energy food contains is usually measured in calories. In 24 hours, an average teenager might use 2,400 calories:

Activity	Hourly energy use	Energy used
8 hours asleep	60 cal	480 cal
8 hours awake but not active, such as sitting reading or watching television	80 cal	640 cal
8 hours physically active, such as walking, playing football, swimming	160 cal	1,280 cal
	Total energy used	2,400 cal

keep on denying themselves food. Anorexics can cause great damage to their bodies. If the body does not get the nutrients it needs, it starts to use up muscle and organ tissue, leading to weakness, organ failure, and eventually death. People with anorexia usually need help from a doctor or specialist to reestablish normal, healthy eating patterns, and they may need to spend time at a residential treatment center.

People who suffer from bulimia also worry about being overweight. They may eat very little for a while, then have a huge binge of overeating, afterward making themselves vomit to get rid of the food. In addition to losing nutrients, repeated vomiting can lead to serious health problems.

Vitamin deficiencies

In the eighteenth century, sailors on long voyages had no fresh vegetables or fruit to eat. Many suffered from a disease called scurvy that made their gums bleed and their teeth fall out. They became weak, their joints became swollen, and they usually died. Eventually, it was found that drinking lime juice kept them free from scurvy. Now we know that citrus fruits, such as limes, lemons, and oranges, contain high amounts of **vitamin** C—and that this prevents scurvy.

Digestion begins when food enters the mouth. Teeth chew and soften food, and it is mixed with **saliva.** The tongue detects different tastes and helps move food around during chewing and swallowing.

Saliva

Saliva is a clear liquid made by the salivary glands in the mouth. There are three pairs of salivary glands: one pair high at the sides near the ears, one pair under the tongue, and a pair under the jaw. In an adult, they can produce more than one quart (one liter) of saliva every day.

Saliva is neutral or slightly **alkaline.** Because it is a base (the opposite of an **acid**), it can work against acids to neutralize them. Saliva can help neutralize the acids produced by **bacteria** in the mouth, which damage teeth and cause decay. It also helps to keep the mouth moist and comfortable. It is about 99 percent water but contains **mucus,** mineral salts, and the **enzyme** salivary amylase as well. The mucus helps to make the food slippery and easy to swallow, and the salivary amylase begins the process of starch digestion.

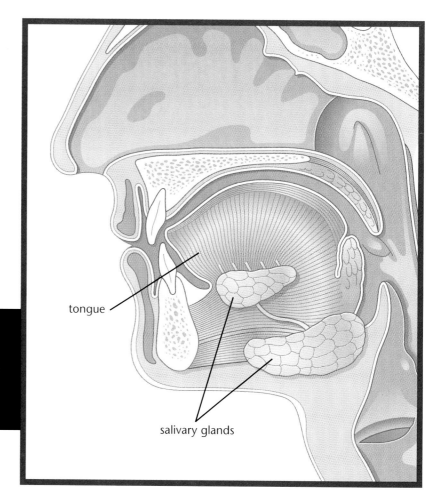

In this diagram of the inside of the mouth, you can see the positions of some of the main salivary glands.

tongue

salivary glands

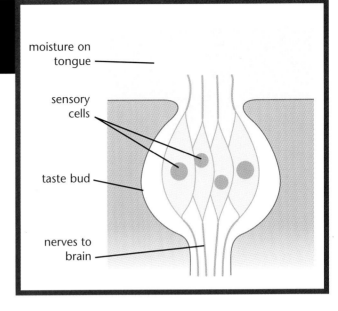

This diagram shows the structure of a single taste bud.

moisture on tongue

sensory cells

taste bud

nerves to brain

Taste

The tongue is mainly muscle. It helps to move food around the mouth when we chew, and it allows us to detect the different tastes of our food. In the upper surface of the tongue, taste-sensitive cells are clustered together in small groups called taste buds. As we chew, chemicals from our food touch our taste buds, and electrical signals are sent to the brain.

There are four main tastes—sweet, salty, sour, and bitter—and scientists used to think that each taste bud could detect only one of these tastes. We now know that every taste bud can detect each taste. Also, scientists now recognize a fifth taste, called umami. It was discovered by Kikunae Ikeda and is triggered by the presence of glutamic acid. This acid is found in meats and other foods, and it is the main ingredient in the chemical monosodium glutamate (MSG), often used as an artificial flavor.

Have you ever noticed that when you have a bad cold, your food seems less tasty than usual? This is because the nose also plays an important role in tasting our food. Cells that are sensitive to smells are situated in the upper lining of the nose. When chemicals in the air pass over the hairs of these cells, electrical signals are sent to the brain, adding information to the signals from the taste buds.

Swallowing

It can be painful if we swallow very hot or very cold food. As food is chewed, it gradually reaches the temperature of the body. When the food has been chewed well and mixed with saliva, it becomes soft and moist and is eventually ready to swallow. Several things happen:
- A flap of cartilage called the epiglottis blocks off the entrance to the windpipe, keeping food from entering the airways.
- The soft palate blocks off the entrance to the nasal cavity.
- The tongue pushes upward and backward against the roof of the mouth, pushing a small lump of food, called a **bolus,** to the back of the mouth.

We usually choose when we begin to swallow, but when the bolus hits the back of the mouth, the rest of the swallow becomes an automatic reaction. The food is forced out of the mouth and into the esophagus.

Babies are usually born without teeth. The first set of teeth, called baby teeth, grow during the first years of life. During childhood, these gradually fall out and are replaced by permanent teeth. The last four molars, called wisdom teeth, often do not appear until the late teens, and sometimes they never appear at all. Our teeth are very important, helping us to bite our food and to chew it so it is ready to swallow.

Baby teeth

The first teeth, sometimes called "milk teeth," usually begin to appear in a baby's first year. They continue to appear at the rate of about one pair each month or two until there are twenty altogether—ten in the upper jaw and ten in the lower jaw. During early childhood, the permanent teeth develop slowly inside the gums. Between the ages of about six and twelve, the permanent teeth emerge and the baby teeth are lost.

Permanent teeth

Adults have 32 teeth, sixteen in each of the upper and lower jaws. Each tooth has two parts: the crown is the part we see above the gum, and the root is hidden inside the gum. If these teeth are lost or damaged, the body cannot replace them.

Teeth with different shapes do different jobs:
- Incisors, at the front of the mouth, are sharp and are good at slicing off pieces of food. We use these when taking a bite from a large piece of food such as an apple.
- Canine teeth, at the sides of the mouth, are pointed, and are good for gripping and tearing food.
- Premolars and molars, at the back of the mouth, have broad bumpy surfaces for crushing and grinding. We use these to chew our food, softening it so it can be mixed with **saliva** and swallowed.

Inside a tooth

Teeth are made up of several layers. The outer layer is a hard, shiny coating called enamel. Beneath this is dentine, a very hard layer like bone. The dentine gets **nutrients** and oxygen from blood vessels that lie in the tooth's soft core, called the pulp. The pulp also contains nerves.

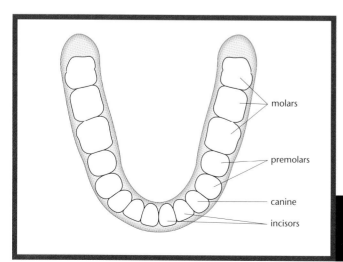

molars

premolars

canine

incisors

This diagram shows the positions of the different types of teeth in an adult mouth.

Teeth and diet

Different creatures have different types of teeth suited to their diets. The large, sharp incisors of rodents such as mice and squirrels allow them to nibble at their food of nuts and seeds. Carnivores such as lions and foxes have strong canines for gripping and tearing flesh. The broad molars of herbivores like sheep and horses can grind large quantities of plant material. Humans are omnivores—that means we eat a mixed diet—so we have some teeth of each type.

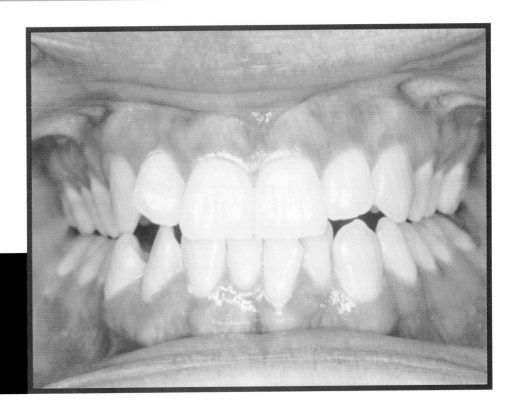

Teeth are not all the same size or shape. Different types of teeth have different functions.

Looking after teeth

Our permanent teeth should last us for the rest of our lives, but we have to help by taking care of them. It makes sense to:

- remember to brush and floss teeth morning and night, removing any scraps of food that remain and eliminating the **bacteria** that cause tooth decay;
- avoid sugary, sticky foods, so that no sugar remains on the teeth for harmful bacteria to feed on;
- visit the dentist regularly so that any problems can be dealt with in the early stages before they become too advanced.

The esophagus, sometimes called the gullet or the foodpipe, carries food from the mouth to the stomach. In an adult, it is about 10 inches (25 centimeters) long, with strong muscular walls that move the food along.

The esophagus is made up of a series of layers. Although there are variations in size and surface details, the basic structure is the same throughout the alimentary canal:

1. The outer layer (called the adventitia or serosa) is a thin layer of connective tissue.
2. Beneath this is a layer of **longitudinal muscle** fibers that stretch the full length of the esophagus.
3. Next comes a layer of **circular muscle** fibers that run in rings around the esophagus.
4. Below this is a thick layer of connective tissue (the submucosa) that contains nerves and blood vessels.
5. The innermost lining of the esophagus, the **mucosa**, produces **mucus** that keeps the food slippery, helping it to slide easily along.

At the center is the space through which the food moves—the lumen. Its irregular shape is made by the folds and wrinkles of the mucosa that surrounds it.

Trained sword swallowers like this one are able to control the natural reflex of the esophagus muscles in order to pass the sword down toward the stomach. Sword swallowing is a life-threatening activity and should be carried out only by skilled, trained professionals. NEVER try this yourself.

Moving food

Food cannot move along by itself. In the esophagus, muscles contract and relax in turn, pushing the food along. These muscle movements ripple along the esophagus like waves. This process of moving food is called **peristalsis,** and it occurs throughout the alimentary canal.

The circular muscles behind the food contract, and the circular muscles in front of the food relax. This squeezes the **bolus** along a little way into the space where the muscles are relaxed. These muscles then contract, and the muscles in front relax, squeezing the food along again. The longitudinal muscles contract too, so a section of the esophagus is shortened, helping to push the bolus forward. Food moves along the esophagus at about 1.6 inches (four centimeters) per second, so it will take about six seconds to travel from your mouth to your stomach.

The strong pressure from the muscles always forces food along the digestive system in the right direction—even if you're standing on your head! The bottom of the esophagus is kept tightly closed by a ring of muscle called the esophageal **sphincter.** This ring relaxes to allow food into the stomach, and then contracts again to close the entrance to the stomach.

Gas

Every time we eat a meal, we swallow air along with our food. This may be released from the stomach by belching. Some air may enter the small intestine and cause a gurgling sound as it travels along. Any remaining excess gas leaves the body through the **anus** as flatulence, usually when we use the toilet.

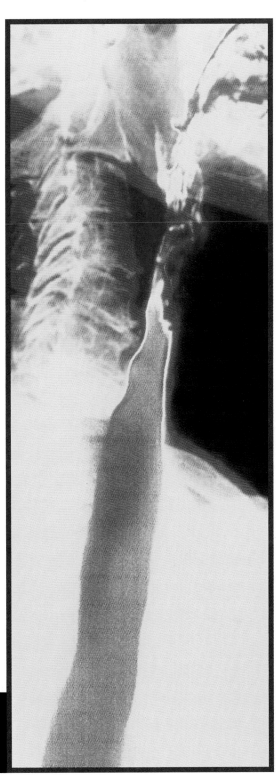

This patient has swallowed barium meal (a substance that shows up on an X-ray). We can clearly see the tube of the esophagus (in red).

STOMACH

The stomach stores food after we eat it. **Digestive** juices produced by the stomach break down the food, turning it into a liquid that is then passed on to the rest of the alimentary canal.

The stomach is a muscular sac that stretches to hold food from a meal. An adult's stomach is about ten inches (25 centimeters) long and is made up of the same layers as the esophagus—a protective outer layer, **longitudinal muscles, circular muscles,** connective tissue, and **mucosa.** When the stomach is empty, the mucosa becomes wrinkled. As you eat, the stomach stretches to hold the food, and these wrinkles gradually disappear.

The mucosa of the stomach contains special glands that make a liquid called **gastric** juice. It produces about 2 quarts (1.9 liters) every day. Gastric juice contains:

- pepsin, an **enzyme** that breaks down **proteins** into smaller **molecules** called peptides
- hydrochloric **acid,** a strong acid that keeps the stomach contents acidic. These acidic conditions help pepsin do its work best. The hydrochloric acid also helps to dissolve **minerals** and kill harmful microorganisms.

This diagram shows the structure of the stomach wall.

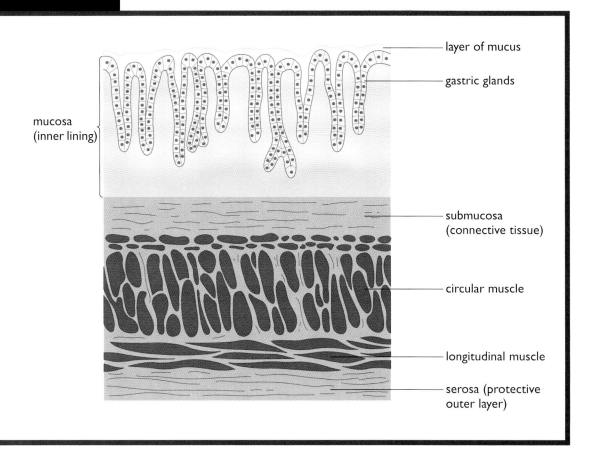

layer of mucus

gastric glands

mucosa (inner lining)

submucosa (connective tissue)

circular muscle

longitudinal muscle

serosa (protective outer layer)

- lipase, an enzyme that breaks down **fats** into **fatty acids**. However, lipase cannot work in the presence of hydrochloric acid, so little fat digestion takes place in the stomach. It occurs in the small intestine instead.
- **mucus,** to help to lubricate the food. Mucus also forms a protective layer covering the inside surface of the stomach, preventing it from being attacked by the acid and enzymes of gastric juice.

Churning food

When food enters the stomach, slow **peristaltic** waves start in the upper area of the stomach, with the muscles of the stomach wall contracting and relaxing about once every twenty seconds. These movements churn the food, mixing it thoroughly with the gastric juice. Different foods stay in the stomach for different lengths of time, depending on the chemicals they contain. Water passes through within a few minutes, while a meal rich in **carbohydrates,** such as pasta, may pass through in about an hour or so. Meals containing fats and proteins, like hamburgers and French fries, may stay in the stomach for 2–5 hours or more.

The stomach churns and mixes the food, eventually turning it into a soupy liquid called **chyme**. The stomach does not absorb any **nutrients** from the food. The peristaltic movements of the stomach muscles squirt chyme out of the stomach, through a ring of muscle called the pyloric **sphincter,** and into the small intestine.

Alcohol and the stomach

Alcohol is not a nutrient and may be absorbed into the bloodstream from both the stomach and the small intestine. The small intestine can absorb it much faster, so the longer the alcohol stays in the stomach, the more slowly it will be absorbed, and the lower the level of alcohol in the blood will be. The stomach also contains an enzyme that breaks down alcohol, so the alcohol is broken down more when it stays in the stomach longer. Drinking alcohol with a fatty meal such as pizza and fries makes the alcohol move into the small intestine more slowly, so more alcohol is broken down while still in the stomach. This means it is absorbed into the blood more slowly, so people feel less intoxicated.

STOMACH PROBLEMS

Everything that we eat and drink passes through the stomach. Most of the time, this processing goes smoothly, but sometimes people experience various stomach problems.

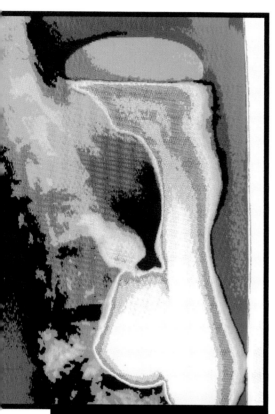

X-rays cannot pass through barium sulfate. If a patient swallows a suspension of barium sulfate (a "barium meal"), the stomach can be seen clearly on an X-ray (here it is yellow orange).

Stomach ulcers

The thick layer of **mucus** lining the stomach usually protects it from attack by **gastric** juice. Sometimes, however, gastric juice can penetrate the mucus and damage the stomach wall. This damage is called a gastric ulcer. If the damage continues, blood vessels in the stomach wall may rupture, letting blood escape into the stomach. A perforated ulcer occurs if a gastric ulcer eats right through the stomach wall, allowing food and digestive juices to escape into the abdomen.

What causes ulcers?

There are a variety of factors that may lead to development of a gastric ulcer, although it is unlikely that any of these things would cause an ulcer on its own. They include smoking, drinking a lot of alcohol, eating irregular or hurried meals, and stress. All of these things may reduce the stomach's defense and repair mechanisms, making it more open to attack by its own hydrochloric **acid.** Some drugs such as aspirin and some steroids may affect the lining of the stomach and increase the risk of developing a gastric ulcer. A **bacterium,** *Helicobacter pylori,* has also been associated with gastric ulcers—it produces **enzymes** that damage the stomach lining.

Symptoms

A gastric ulcer usually causes pain in the upper abdomen about an hour after a meal. The person may feel sick, and vomiting often helps to relieve the pain. To find out exactly what is wrong, doctors can pass an endoscope down the throat and into the stomach. This flexible fiber-optic tube can help them to examine the internal walls of the stomach. Alternatively, a barium X-ray can give an indication of the problem. Antacid tablets can ease the pain by neutralizing the stomach acid. A doctor can also prescribe drugs to reduce the amount of stomach acid being made, or to help to form a protective covering over the ulcer. Sometimes an operation is needed to help to repair the damage.

Gastric ulcers that are not treated may eventually begin to bleed, causing **anemia**. In very severe cases, they can be fatal.

Indigestion

Usually, the **digestive** system works without our being aware of it. Sometimes, though, there is pain after eating a meal, together with a bloated, sick feeling. We call this condition indigestion. It is not dangerous and usually goes away after a while.

Several things may cause indigestion. Certain foods, such as curry, onions, and cucumber, may lead to indigestion. These foods may remain in the stomach longer than others and can produce excess acid. In other cases, indigestion may be due to overeating, eating hurriedly, feeling stressed, and drinking too much alcohol. Vomiting often gets rid of the pain, and antacid tablets can also help.

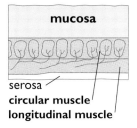

stomach lining is healthy—mucus produced, protecting stomach wall

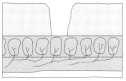

ulcer beginning— mucus layer eroded

ulcer bleeding as stomach wall and tissues are eroded

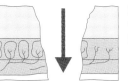

perforated ulcer— complete erosion of part of stomach wall

These diagrams show how an ulcer may develop in the stomach.

Heartburn

The esophageal **sphincter** usually remains tightly closed to keep the stomach contents from moving back into the esophagus. Sometimes, however, the acid contents of the stomach do escape into the esophagus, causing a burning sensation as they irritate the esophageal lining. This condition is known as heartburn. It is not serious, and antacid tablets can relieve the pain.

Vomiting

Vomiting is the body's way of getting rid of harmful substances. It is a mechanism that helps us to partly—or completely—empty the stomach. Several things happen when we vomit:

- The top of the stomach goes into spasm, and **peristaltic** waves start to operate in reverse, pushing food backwards (the wrong way) along the alimentary canal.
- The body of the stomach and the esophageal sphincter relax.
- The upper part of the small intestine also goes into spasm, forcing its contents back into the stomach.
- The **glottis** closes, and the soft palate rises to keep vomit from entering the airways.
- Abdominal pressure squeezes the stomach, forcing its contents back through the esophagus and out through the mouth.

SMALL INTESTINE

The small intestine connects the stomach and the large intestine. In an adult, it is about 1.5 inches (4 centimeters) in diameter. Its total length is about twenty feet (six meters), but it is looped and folded so it fits inside the abdomen. It is subdivided into three main areas: the duodenum, jejunum, and ileum. Food may remain in the small intestine for between one and six hours. **Digestion** of food and absorption of **nutrients** takes place within the small intestine, leaving mainly waste matter to pass into the large intestine.

When the **chyme** leaves the stomach, it passes into the duodenum. This is about 10 inches (25 centimeters) long and is shaped like the letter C. In the duodenum, digestive juices from the liver and **pancreas** are added to the chyme:

- **Bile** is a watery, **alkaline** fluid made by the liver and stored in the gallbladder. It does not contain any **enzymes**, but bile salts act on **fats** to break them up into small droplets.
- Pancreatic juice from the pancreas contains several enzymes. Proteases break down **proteins** into peptides and **amino acids**. Pancreatic amylase digests starch, converting it into maltose. Lipase digests fats, breaking them down into **fatty acids** and **glycerol**. These enzymes do not work well in an acidic environment, so pancreatic juice also contains an alkali to neutralize the **acid** in chyme.

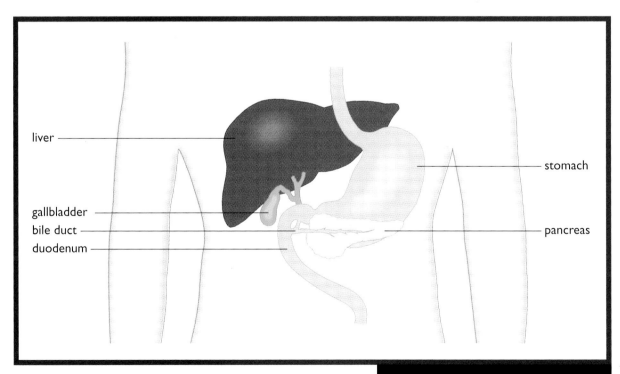

liver

stomach

gallbladder
bile duct
duodenum

pancreas

This diagram shows the duodenum and its connections with the liver and pancreas.

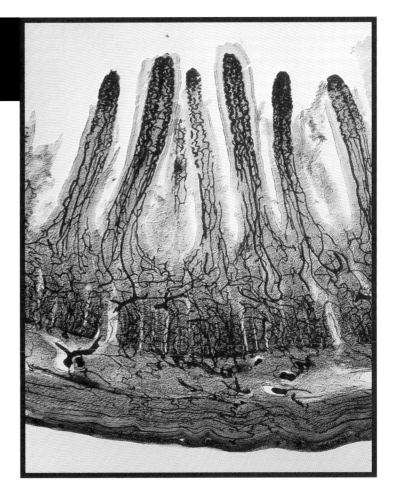

This photomicrograph shows the fingerlike villi in part of the small intestine wall.

The small intestine connects the stomach and the large intestine. In an adult, it is about 1.5 inches (4 centimeters) in diameter. Its total length is about twenty feet (six meters), but it is looped and folded so it fits inside the abdomen. It is subdivided into three main areas: the duodenum, jejunum, and ileum. Food may remain in the small intestine for between one and six hours. **Digestion** of food and absorption of **nutrients** takes place within the small intestine, leaving mainly waste matter to pass into the large intestine.

When the **chyme** leaves the stomach, it passes into the duodenum. This is about 10 inches (25 centimeters) long and is shaped like the letter C. In the duodenum, digestive juices from the liver and **pancreas** are added to the chyme:

- **Bile** is a watery, **alkaline** fluid made by the liver and stored in the gallbladder. It does not contain any **enzymes,** but bile salts act on **fats** to break them up into small droplets.
- Pancreatic juice from the pancreas contains several enzymes. Proteases break down **proteins** into peptides and **amino acids.** Pancreatic amylase digests starch, converting it into maltose. Lipase digests fats, breaking them down into **fatty acids** and **glycerol.** These enzymes do not work well in an acidic environment, so pancreatic juice also contains an alkali to neutralize the **acid** in chyme.

From the duodenum, the chyme passes into the jejunum (about 8 feet/2.5 meters long) and then into the ileum (about 1.5 feet/3.5 meters long). Glands in the walls of the small intestine produce a dilute **mucus** and salt solution that provides lubrication and a watery environment for the rest of the digestive processes to take place. Digestive enzymes are also produced by glands (called "crypts of Lieberkühn") in the small intestine wall. These enzymes complete the

Liquid waste from which **nutrients** have been absorbed enters the large intestine. Water is removed in the large intestine and solid waste passes on to the rectum, where it is stored until we use the toilet.

The large intestine is three to six feet (one to two meters) long—about one-sixth of the small intestine's length. It is called the large intestine because it is about 2.5 inches (6 centimeters) in diameter, compared to 1.5 inches (4 centimeters) for the small intestine. Its main sections form most of a rectangle shape, surrounding the small intestine.

Cecum

Liquid waste passes into the first section, the cecum, through a **sphincter**-like structure called the ileocecal **valve**. This is usually partly closed, allowing liquid through in a slow, steady trickle. The open end of the cecum leads into the next section of the large intestine, the colon. Attached to the cecum is a small narrow tube, the appendix, that does not play any part in **digestion** but may have some function as part of the body's **immune system.**

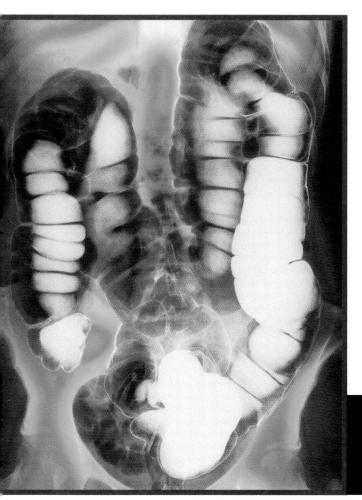

Colon

The next section of the large intestine is called the colon. Its wall has no villi or folds, and no **enzymes** are produced. Absorptive cells remove water from the waste, and goblet cells produce **mucus** for lubrication, helping waste slide easily along the large intestine. Liquid waste is continuously pushed along the colon by slow **peristaltic** waves. The muscular walls of the colon generate between three and twelve of these waves each minute. Additionally, three or four times a day, usually during or after a meal, an extra strong peristaltic wave sweeps along the colon, forcing the contents into the rectum.

In this colored X-ray, the large intestine is shown in yellow. The cecum (left) leads to the colon (center and left) making a U-shaped loop.

This diagram shows how the main sections of the large intestine are curved into a rectangular shape.

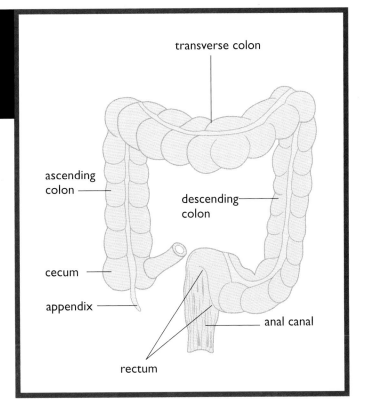

transverse colon

ascending colon

descending colon

cecum

appendix

anal canal

rectum

Although we generally think of **bacteria** as being harmful, we rely on the bacteria that live in the large intestine to complete the breakdown of waste. They convert any remaining **carbohydrates** and **proteins** into simpler substances and release some gases. **Vitamins** K and B_{12} are produced by the action of bacteria and are absorbed into the blood.

Waste

Solid waste is called **feces**. It contains water, some **minerals**, waste products from blood and the intestinal walls, bacteria and bacterial products, unabsorbed material, and indigestible material such as fiber. An S-shaped bend leads from the end of the colon into the rectum. As feces collect in the rectum, the rectal walls stretch, stimulating stretch receptors in the wall. Rectal muscles contract, shortening the rectum and increasing the pressure inside. The waste passes into the anal canal, where there is a rich network of blood vessels. At the end of the anal canal is the **anus**, ending in two sphincter muscles, both of which are usually closed. When we use the toilet, voluntary contractions of the diaphragm and abdominal muscles open the sphincters, and waste is pushed out of the body through the anus.

Appendicitis

Any blockage in the appendix can lead to inflammation called appendicitis. It usually causes an uncomfortable feeling in the abdomen that eventually becomes severe. A hundred years ago, appendicitis was rare. Doctors think that it is becoming increasingly common because our diet generally contains much less fiber than that of previous generations. A person with appendicitis usually has an operation to remove the appendix, to prevent it from bursting and spreading infection inside the abdomen. Because the appendix does not carry out any important function, we can live quite happily without it.

INTESTINAL PROBLEMS

Everybody has probably experienced an intestinal problem at some time. Some problems are mild and pass quickly, while others are more serious and may last for a long time.

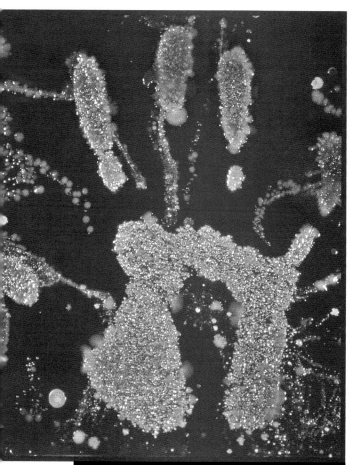

This handprint shows the bacteria that can develop if we do not wash our hands!

Diarrhea

If waste moves through the large intestine too quickly, water cannot be properly absorbed. Soft, watery **feces** forms, and you usually feel an uncontrollable need to rush to the toilet. Diarrhea may be caused by infection from **bacteria** or a **virus**, sometimes as a result of eating spoiled or infected food. It can also be caused by toxic substances such as some weed killers, by some medications, and even by extreme nervousness or stress.

Diarrhea that continues for some time can lead to dehydration. Some **nutrients**, like salts, are also lost because they pass through the alimentary canal too quickly to be absorbed. This is not always serious in adults but can be very dangerous in young children.

A good way to lower the risk of diarrhea from bacterial infection is to practice good hygiene, both in food preparation and personal behavior—such as washing your hands after using the toilet.

Constipation

If waste moves through the large intestine too slowly, too much water may be absorbed from it. This results in hard feces and difficulty in **defecation**. Constipation may be caused by a variety of factors, including a lack of fiber in the diet, stress, some drugs, or too little exercise. A mild laxative can speed up the movement of waste through the large intestine and may help to relieve the problem.

Inflammatory diseases

The intestine may become inflamed, causing cramping pains and fever. If the inflammation is only in the large intestine, it is called ulcerative colitis. If it extends to other places in the alimentary canal, especially the ileum, it may be called Crohn's disease. A single cause has not been proved, but some doctors think it may be due to an infection or **food allergy.** In mild cases, simple diarrhea remedies and **vitamin** supplements may bring relief. In more serious cases, drugs such as steroids may be given to suppress the **immune system.**

Irritable Bowel Syndrome

People suffering from irritable bowel syndrome (IBS) have alternating bouts of diarrhea and constipation, together with abdominal cramps and pains, and a feeling of sickness and loss of appetite. This condition is often associated with stress and depression. Changing the diet to include more fiber can sometimes help, and some drugs are available to help to control the symptoms.

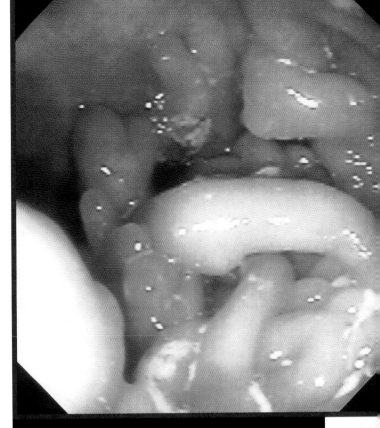

This is part of an intestine affected by Crohn's disease, a condition that can seriously affect the digestive system.

Hernia

A hernia is a lump that arises when a loop of intestine protrudes through the abdominal wall lining. These are relatively common and may be due to an inborn weakness, a serious and persistent cough, or the strain of lifting heavy objects. Hernias may be treated by surgical repair or by the wearing of a special belt.

Hemorrhoids

These are enlarged veins inside the **anal** canal, where the spongy tissues have a rich supply of blood vessels. As the sores swell and get larger, they lead to bleeding and can be painful. A warm bath can ease the discomfort, and a diet high in fiber can make defecation easier. Treatments can include freezing the hemorrhoids, restricting their blood supply, or giving injections to make them shrivel. An operation may sometimes be necessary to remove them completely.

Colon cancer

Colon cancer has become increasingly common, possibly because our diets contain less fiber and more animal **fat** than in the past. This cancer may cause diarrhea or constipation, bleeding from the rectum, and dull pain. If caught early, many cases can be cured, but surgery is sometimes necessary.

# LIVER

The liver is the largest organ in the body, with a mass of about 3 to 4 pounds (1.4–1.8 kilograms). It lies just below the diaphragm, a sheet of muscle that separates the chest from the abdomen. The liver has two lobes: the right is six times bigger than the left and lies in front of the right kidney. The liver helps to regulate and control many of the body's systems.

Inside the liver

The liver is made up of many small structures called lobules. Each lobule has six sides and is about 0.04 inch (one millimeter) in diameter. Blood and **bile** flow through the lobules in opposite directions.

Blood supply

Blood is brought to the liver in the **hepatic artery** and hepatic portal **vein**. The liver does not contain **capillaries**, but each lobule has a series of spaces that the blood passes through. Liver cells take up oxygen, **nutrients**, and toxic substances. The blood picks up products made by the liver and nutrients to be transported elsewhere in the body.

What does the liver do?

The conditions inside our bodies—such as our temperature, chemical levels, and water level—need to be kept constant. The regulation of this internal environment is called homeostasis, and most of this process is carried out by the liver.

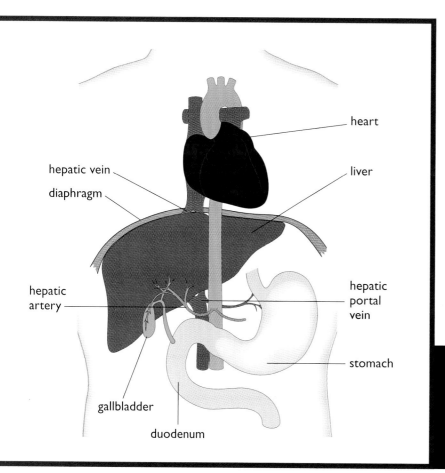

hepatic vein
diaphragm
hepatic artery
gallbladder
duodenum
heart
liver
hepatic portal vein
stomach

This diagram shows the position of the liver in the body, as well as the blood vessels and organs that surround it.

The main functions of the liver include:

- regulation of blood sugar levels: When the concentration of sugar in the blood is high, the liver removes **glucose** from the blood and stores it as **glycogen.** When the concentration drops, the reverse happens.
- **fat** metabolism: The liver breaks down **fatty acids** and builds up new substances from them. Every day, the liver produces about one quart (one liter) of bile, a substance that is essential for the **digestion** of fats in the small intestine.

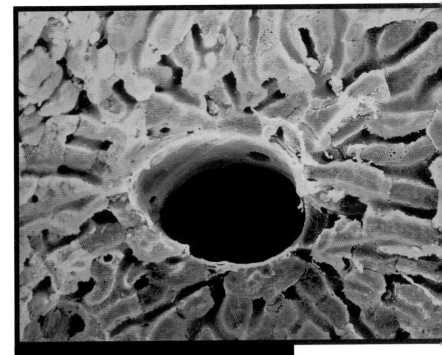

Here you can see a lobule of the liver, magnified many times.

- **protein** metabolism: When **amino acids** are broken down, ammonia is produced. This chemical is toxic, so the liver converts it into urea, a harmless chemical that is **excreted** in urine. The liver also produces some amino acids and proteins that are needed in the blood.
- regulating **vitamins:** The liver **synthesizes** vitamin A from carotene, a chemical found in some fruits and vegetables (especially carrots). The liver also activates vitamin D and stores many other vitamins until they are needed.
- regulating **minerals:** The liver removes iron from the **hemoglobin** of broken-down red blood cells. Hemoglobin is vital for the transport of oxygen, so the liver stores it until it can be used to make new red blood cells. The liver also stores other minerals until they are needed.
- regulating toxins: Harmful chemicals such as alcohol, drugs, poisons, environmental pollutants, and surplus **hormones** are removed from the blood and broken down by **enzymes** in the liver.
- temperature control: The many chemical reactions that are carried out inside the liver generate heat. This warms the blood as it passes through, and the blood carries the heat to the rest of the body, helping to maintain a constant body temperature.

Gallbladder

The gallbladder is a small, pear-shaped organ that lies under a lobe of the liver. It stores bile and makes it more concentrated by absorbing water from it. The gallbladder also produces **mucus** for lubrication.

LIVER PROBLEMS

The liver is a complex organ, continuously carrying out a large variety of chemical reactions. It is responsible for vital functions without which the body would not survive, but it can be damaged by poisons, drugs, and infections.

Cirrhosis

In this chronic liver disease, normal liver cells are destroyed and replaced by fibrous tissue, making the liver hard and unable to function efficiently. The most common cause of cirrhosis is heavy consumption of alcohol over a long period of time. In the early stages, there may be no symptoms. As the disease progresses, though, **hormones** may accumulate as the liver fails to break them down, and **jaundice** may occur as **bile** builds up in the blood. The abdomen may swell, body muscles may become weak, and there may be internal bleeding. Eventually, the circulation in the liver is blocked, leading to liver failure and death. However, the liver is able to repair itself, as long as it is not too badly damaged. If cirrhosis is detected at an early stage, and the patient stops drinking alcohol, the damage can often be repaired.

Hepatitis

Hepatitis is usually caused by infection by a **virus,** resulting in inflammation of the liver. It can affect people of all ages and is highly infectious. There are three main types: hepatitis A, B, and C.

Hepatitis A is often spread in contaminated food or water. It is usually a relatively mild disease, causing no long-term problems.

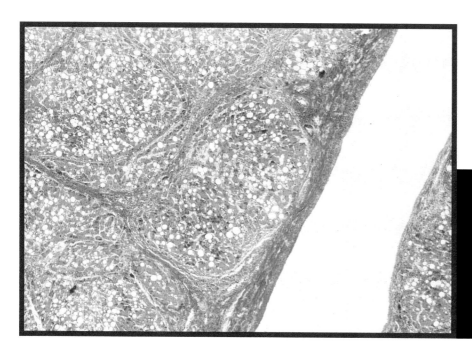

Fibrous scar tissue (green) has developed around the lobules in this patient's liver. This damage has been caused by too much alcohol.

Hepatitis B and hepatitis C may be spread through infected blood or sexual contact. They are common among drug addicts who may share hypodermic needles. Babies of infected pregnant women may also develop these forms of hepatitis.

In some cases, the symptoms of infection by hepatitis B or C may not even be noticed, although blood tests can detect the infection and show which virus is involved. Hepatitis B is a serious disease that can sometimes be fatal, but scientists have discovered a vaccine for it. However, there is no vaccine for hepatitis C, which can lead to permanent liver damage.

Jaundice

When old red blood cells are broken down, a yellow bile pigment is released. The liver usually removes this pigment from the blood and **excretes** it in bile, so the levels of bile pigment in the blood are normally very low. If the amounts in the blood rise, the skin becomes yellowish, and the patient may feel more tired than usual. This condition, known as jaundice, is common in newborn babies, because their livers are not mature enough to cope with the breakdown of red blood cells.

This X-ray shows that the patient's gallbladder (the red "pear" shape) contains many gallstones (green).

Gallstones

If bile contains too much cholesterol or not enough bile salts, the cholesterol may crystallize to form gallstones. At first, these may not cause any problems, but as they get bigger they may block the bile duct. Then bile cannot leave the gallbladder, so fat cannot be **digested** properly, and jaundice may occur. In some cases, eating a fat-free diet can control the problem. Alternatively, some drugs can be used to dissolve the gallstones, or lithotripsy (shock waves) can shatter them. They may also be surgically removed—in some patients the entire gallbladder may be taken out. After treatment, the patient can resume a perfectly normal life.

PANCREAS

Just behind the stomach lies a small, pinkish-gray organ called the **pancreas.** This produces pancreatic juice containing important digestive **enzymes.** It also produces **hormones,** including **insulin** and glucagon, which help to regulate the amount of sugar in the blood.

In an adult, the pancreas is about 6 inches (15 centimeters) long and 1 inch (2.5 centimeters) thick. The cells of the pancreas need a good blood supply to allow them to function and to carry away the hormones they produce.

When taste buds in the mouth detect food, messages are sent to the brain. The brain then sends messages to the pancreas, stimulating the production of pancreatic juice in preparation for **digestion** of the food.

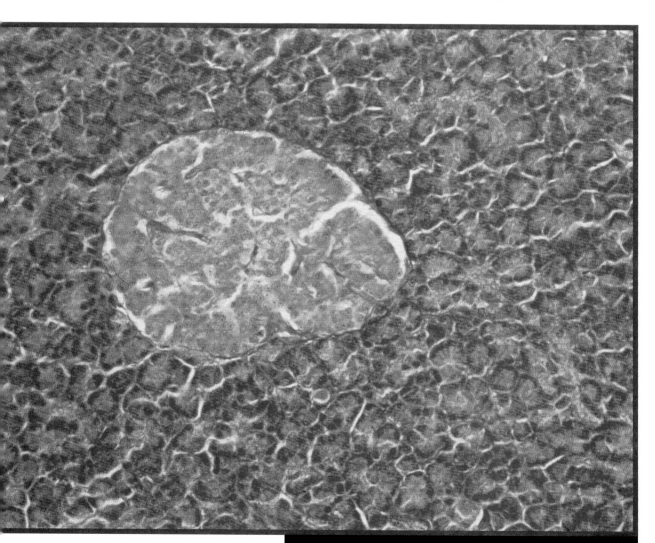

Here, you can see how the cells inside the pancreas are arranged in an islet of Langerhans.

The majority of cells in the pancreas are exocrine cells, seen here magnified many times.

Pancreatic cells

There are two main types of cell in the pancreas: exocrine cells and endocrine cells. About 99 percent of the pancreatic cells are exocrine cells. These are arranged in groups, and they produce pancreatic juice. They are clustered together around tiny ducts that form a network to carry the pancreatic juice away. These ducts eventually join together to form two large ducts. The larger of these, the pancreatic duct, connects to the common **bile** duct from the gallbladder and liver, and it carries pancreatic juice and bile to the duodenum (part of the small intestine). The smaller duct is the accessory duct. It leads straight from the pancreas into the duodenum, about one inch (two to three centimeters) higher than the pancreatic duct.

The other one percent of cells in the pancreas are endocrine cells. These cells are clustered together into small groups called islets of Langerhans. There are four different types of cells in each islet, each producing a different hormone that is released into the blood. These hormones interact with each other, and this interaction helps to regulate the amounts of each that are produced. Blood components and intestinal contents also play a part in regulating the production of these hormones.

DIABETES

There are several types of diabetes, all causing problems with control of blood sugar levels. Diabetes is a major cause of death in developed countries, more because of its side effects than the disorder itself.

As long as they are careful, diabetics can live a normal life. The rower Steve Redgrave did not let diabetes stop him.

Controlling blood sugar levels

Blood sugar levels are controlled by the interaction of the liver and **pancreas.** The pancreas produces the **hormones insulin** and glucagon. If the level of sugar in the blood begins to drop, the pancreas produces glucagon. This enters the blood and is carried to the liver, where it stimulates liver cells to convert some of their stored glycogen into **glucose.** This is released into the blood, and the blood sugar level soon climbs back to normal.

If the amount of sugar in the blood rises above normal, the pancreas produces insulin. This then enters the blood and is carried to the liver, where it stimulates liver cells to remove glucose from the blood and store it as glycogen. This lowers the blood sugar level.

This feedback system usually operates effectively to keep blood sugar levels within the correct limits. In patients with diabetes, however, the system does not work well, and they are unable to control their blood sugar levels.

Types of diabetes

There are two main types of diabetes:

- *Type I (insulin-dependent)*
  This usually begins before the age of twenty and continues through the rest of the patient's life. In this type, the **immune system** attacks and destroys the cells in the pancreas, preventing insulin production. Excess glucose builds up in the blood and is **excreted** in the urine. The patient may produce up to five gallons (twenty liters) of urine a day and must drink a lot of water to replace this fluid. The body behaves as if it is starving. Waste products called ketones build up in the blood and make the blood more **acidic**—if left untreated, this situation may eventually cause death. Regular injections of insulin keep blood sugar levels steady and minimize complications.

Side effects of Type I diabetes include weight loss, heart and blood problems, loss of vision, and kidney damage.

- *Type II (non-insulin dependent)*
  Type II diabetes accounts for 90 percent of diabetics. It usually affects overweight people over the age of 35. Patients have plenty of insulin, but their cells have become less sensitive to it. The symptoms are usually milder than those of Type I. Some patients may need insulin injections, but many can control their high glucose levels with a low-sugar diet, regular exercise, and weight loss.

Other types of diabetes are less common and may have a variety of causes.

Hyperinsulinism

This condition, also called hypoglycemia, can occur if a patient injects too much insulin. The blood sugar level falls too low, and brain cells do not have enough glucose to function normally. Within minutes, the patient feels shaky, and he or she may become unconscious or even die unless glucose is given quickly.

Type I diabetics lack insulin, so they need to inject it regularly.

Hyperglycemia

Hyperglycemia can occur if a patient's blood sugar level rises too high. It is a much slower process than hypoglycemia, taking several hours to develop and several hours to get back to normal.

Living with diabetes

Although the outlook for diabetics has improved dramatically, the disease is still not an easy one to live with. Controlling blood sugar levels requires careful discipline, and this can be very frustrating—especially if you are a teenager just wanting to be the same as your friends. A dietician can help you plan what to eat and what to avoid—reducing **fats**, avoiding sugar and salt, and eating regular meals are all important. The amount of food you take in must be carefully balanced with the amount of exercise that you do. Doctors will give instructions about how often the blood or urine should be tested to show the sugar levels, and about how much insulin must be injected and how often.

KIDNEYS

We have two reddish organs called kidneys, each about 4 to 5 inches (10 to 12 centimeters) long and about 2.5 inches (5 centimeters) wide. They lie one on each side of the spine just above the waist and are partly protected by the lower ribs. The right kidney is a little lower than the left because the liver takes up more abdominal space on the right of the body. The kidneys' main function is to filter the blood, removing waste chemicals and water, and producing a liquid called urine that is passed to the bladder. After filtering out unwanted chemicals, the kidneys then return salts, other chemicals, and water to the blood, ensuring that the right level of each is maintained.

Blood supply

In order to filter the blood, the kidneys need a good blood supply. Blood travels to each kidney through the **renal arteries** and leaves through the renal **veins**. Inside the kidney, the arteries branch many times to form a network of smaller vessels. Approximately 1.3 quarts (1.2 liters) of blood flow through the kidneys every minute, and all the blood in the body passes through them about 300 times every day!

Our kidneys are extremely efficient. Together, they are able to filter more blood than the body really needs them to. A single kidney is able to filter enough blood on its own. We can survive and live a healthy, active life with just one kidney.

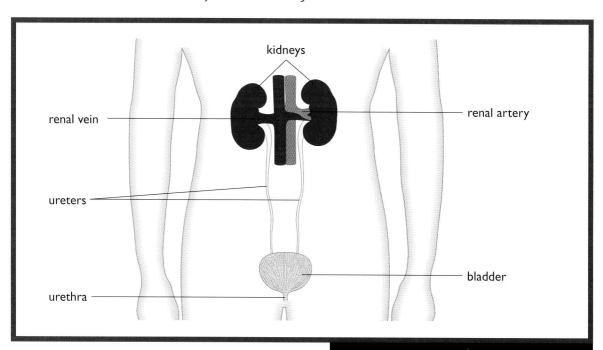

We have two kidneys, one on either side of the spine above the waist.

This diagram shows the internal structure of a kidney.

Kidney structure

Each kidney has a transparent outer membrane that anchors it to the abdominal wall. Below this is a layer of **fat** that acts as a cushion to protect the kidney from damage.

If a kidney is cut in half from top to bottom, three different areas can be seen:

- At the center of the kidney is a large space called the pelvis, where urine collects. The pelvis is connected to a narrow tube, called a ureter, that carries the urine from the kidney to the bladder.
- The middle layer of the kidney is a pale area called the medulla. This is made up of eight to eighteen cone-shaped areas, and it contains ducts that carry urine to the pelvis.
- The darker outer layer, the cortex, is where the blood is filtered. Here, the renal arteries branch into smaller vessels called arterioles. Each arteriole leads to a glomerulus, a group of blood vessels coiled into a knot. Around each glomerulus is a renal capsule (sometimes called a Bowman's capsule) that leads to a renal tubule. These eventually join collecting ducts that pass through the medulla, opening into the pelvis at the top of a pyramid shape. The cortex of a kidney contains thousands of glomeruli. One glomerulus—with its renal capsule, tubule, and **capillaries**—is called a nephron.

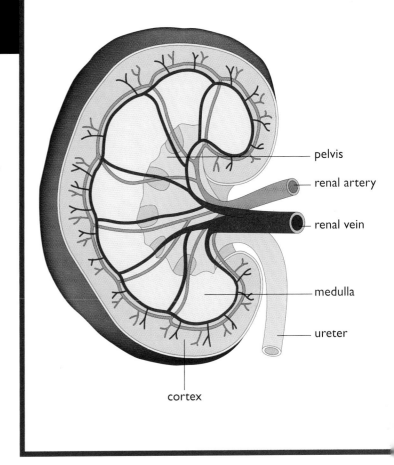

pelvis
renal artery
renal vein
medulla
ureter
cortex

Kidney transplant

A patient's diseased kidney may be removed and replaced with a healthy one from another person. The patient needs to take drugs to ensure that his or her body does not reject the new kidney. Unfortunately, the waiting list for kidneys is long, and patients may wait years before a suitable kidney becomes available.

WHAT HAPPENS IN THE KIDNEYS?

It is in the nephrons that the basic functions of the kidney are carried out. Blood is filtered, unwanted substances are removed, and useful substances are returned to the blood. This maintains the correct levels of fluid and chemicals in the blood and produces urine so that waste can leave the body.

Ultrafiltration

The glomerulus and its **capillaries** are the places where ultrafiltration occurs. In this process, various waste substances are removed from the blood. Blood enters the glomerulus through a capillary. The capillary leaving the glomerulus is narrower than the one entering it, so the pressure inside the glomerulus is raised. This forces fluid out of the blood and through the capillary wall. Blood cells and plasma **proteins** are retained, because they are too large to pass through the capillary wall. The fluid that passes out by **diffusion** is mainly water and dissolved salts, **glucose**, urea, and uric **acid.** This fluid collects in the **renal** capsule.

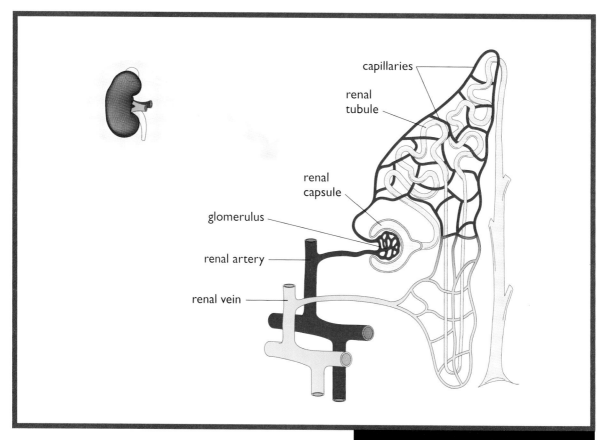

capillaries

renal tubule

renal capsule

glomerulus

renal artery

renal vein

These pictures show what the internal structure of a kidney looks like when magnified.

Selective reabsorption and urine production

In the process of selective reabsorption, certain substances are added back to the blood. This takes place as the fluid collected in the renal capsule trickles down the renal tubule.

As the fluid flows through the tubule, substances that the body needs are absorbed back into the blood. Water, glucose, and some salts are taken back, to maintain the correct levels in the blood. Any water, salts, and other substances not needed by the body pass on down the tubule, together with urea and uric acid. This remaining fluid, the liquid we call urine, then passes through the collecting duct and eventually reaches the pelvis of the kidney. From there, it leaves the kidney through the ureter.

Urine tests

Urine can contain different amounts of different substances, depending in part on how much of each the body needed to reabsorb. Measuring the amounts of some substances contained in the urine can provide important information about your health. Too much glucose in the urine can be a sign of diabetes, while the presence of protein in urine may be a sign of kidney failure. Pregnancy tests detect a **hormone** (human chorionic gonadotropin, or HCG) that is produced by a fertilized egg and **excreted** in the mother's urine within a couple of weeks of conception.

How much urine?

Normally, we produce about 1 to 1.6 quarts (1 to 1.5 liters) of urine every day. This is affected by the amount of water we drink and the amount that we sweat. If we drink a lot, we produce more urine, but the amounts of chemicals to be filtered out remains the same, so the urine is very dilute. If we sweat a lot, we produce much less urine. Again, the same amounts of chemicals have to be filtered out, so the urine is more concentrated. Some substances, such as caffeine and alcohol, are diuretics—they can increase the amount of urine produced. Dilute urine is a very pale, almost colorless liquid. The more concentrated it is, the darker and stronger the color.

KIDNEY PROBLEMS

There are a variety of things that can affect the efficient functioning of the kidneys. Some problems may affect just one kidney, while other problems may affect both. If one kidney fails, the other is usually able to cope with the extra work. If both fail, a patient has to rely on mechanical methods to clean the blood.

Kidney stones

Stones are formed when crystals of salts present in urine solidify into **insoluble** lumps. If these settle in narrow tubes, such as the ureters, they can cause violent, stabbing pains. Kidney stones can be surgically removed, but a newer, alternative technique for their removal is "shock wave lithotripsy." This treatment involves firing brief, high-intensity sound waves at the stones, eventually shattering them into tiny fragments that are carried away in the urine.

Bacterial infections

Bacterial infections can affect any of the tissues of the kidneys. They are most commonly caused by **bacteria** such as *Escherichia coli* (*E.coli*). This bacterium is often spread through contaminated food products. Diarrhea is one common symptom. Treatment with **antibiotics** usually brings the infection under control quickly.

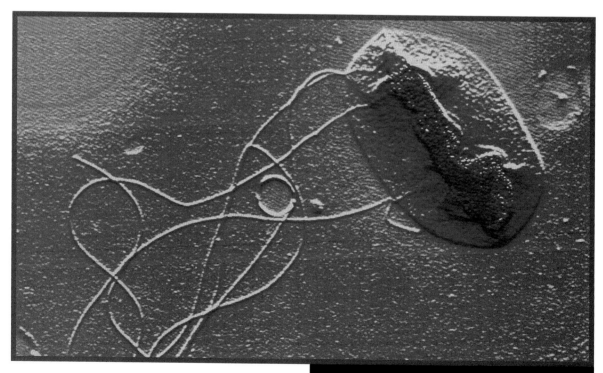

This *E.coli* bacterium can cause some kidney infections.

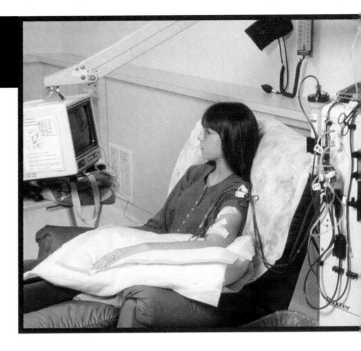

This girl has kidney failure and is using a dialysis machine to cleanse her blood.

Cancer of the kidney

Kidney cancer is much more common in men than in women, and it usually occurs between the ages of 50 and 60. If the cancer is detected early, the kidney can be removed, followed by **radiation** and **chemotherapy.** However, if cancer has already spread to other parts of the body, treatment is not always successful.

Kidney defects

Some people are born with kidney defects. People may have only one kidney, two kidneys fused together, two ureters from each kidney, cysts inside the kidneys, or kidneys in the wrong place within the abdomen. Each individual case is different—some defects may need treatment, while others will not cause any problems and may go unnoticed for years.

Kidney failure

This may be sudden (acute), or may develop slowly over several years (chronic). There are a variety of causes, including heart attack, build-up of toxic chemicals, kidney blockage, and kidney inflammation. A wide range of symptoms may be seen, but the main one is a significant reduction in the amount of urine produced.

Treating kidney failure: dialysis

If a patient's kidneys are unable to filter blood properly, a dialysis machine, or "artificial kidney," may be used. This pumps blood from an **artery** through a series of tubes made from an absorbent membrane. A solution called dialysis fluid is on the other side of the membrane, and as blood flows along, the salts and waste products move out of the blood by **diffusion,** passing through the membrane and into the dialysis fluid. The cleansed blood then goes back to the body. Each cycle of dialysis takes several hours, and most patients need treatment two or three times every week.

BLADDER AND URINATION

The bladder is a sac that collects urine from the kidneys and holds it until we urinate. Urination is an efficient method of removing the waste products in urine from the body.

Ureters

The ureters are narrow tubes that carry urine from the kidneys to the bladder. Each ureter is 10 to 12 inches (25–30 centimeters) long, and 0.04 to 0.4 inch (1 to 10 millimeters) in diameter. Urine is forced along the ureters by **peristaltic** waves that occur one to five times every minute, depending on how fast urine is being produced.

The ureters enter the bladder, one at each side. Before they open to the inside of the bladder, they pass through the bladder wall at an oblique, or slanted, angle. This design acts as a check valve, allowing urine to flow into the bladder but preventing it from flowing backward into the body.

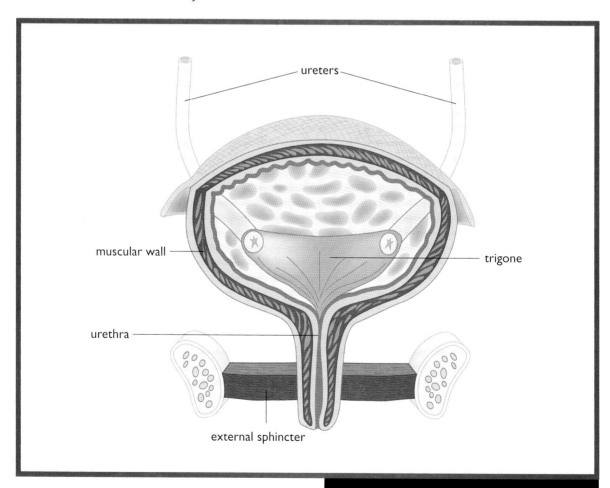

This diagram shows the internal structure of the bladder.

Bladder

The bladder is a hollow, stretchy organ, held in place by the folds of the **peritoneum.** Its shape depends on how much urine it contains. If it is empty, it is collapsed, like an empty balloon; when partly full, it is spherical; when completely full, it is pear-shaped.

Urethra

The urethra is a tube of smooth muscle that carries urine from the bladder out of the body. It is about 1.5 inches (4 centimeters) long in a female, running from the bladder and opening just in front of the vagina. In males, the urethra is about eight inches (twenty centimeters) long, running from the bladder along the length of the penis, to open at the tip of the penis. A muscular ring around the urethra—a **sphincter**—controls the release of urine.

Urination

On average, an adult's bladder can hold 24–27 fluid ounces (700–800 milliliters) of urine, but we usually feel more comfortable emptying it when it is about half full. When the bladder contains ten to 13.5 fluid ounces (300–400 milliliters) of urine, the pressure inside it increases. Stretch receptors in the bladder wall send signals to the spinal cord, triggering a reflex reaction. This makes muscles in the bladder wall contract, and the urethral sphincter relaxes. Urine is forced out of the bladder and through the urethra. As children, we learn to control this reflex and can delay urination for a limited period.

Incontinence

Incontinence, or involuntary release of urine, is normal in young children because they have not learned to control the reflex reaction. Adults may also suffer from incontinence, often as a result of physical stresses such as coughing, sneezing, laughing, exercising, and even pregnancy. These can all increase abdominal pressure, causing leakage from the bladder. Incontinence can also be due to injury, aging, disease, and the effects of some drugs.

Cystitis

Cystitis, or inflammation of the bladder, is usually caused by the **bacterium** *Escherichia coli (E.coli),* and is much more common in women than in men. The first sign is a tingling or burning sensation when urinating, which gradually gets worse and more painful. **Antibiotics** may be used to kill the bacteria. Drinking plenty of water, eating a healthy diet, and maintaining good personal hygiene can all help to reduce the likelihood of cystitis occurring.

WHAT CAN GO WRONG WITH MY DIGESTIVE SYSTEM?

This book has explained the different parts of the digestive system, telling why it is important and how it can be damaged by injury and illness. These pages summarize some of the problems that can affect young people. The table also gives you information about how each problem is treated.

Many problems can also be avoided by good health behavior. This is called prevention. Exercising regularly and getting plenty of rest are important, as is eating the right kinds of foods. A balanced diet is particularly important for maintaining a healthy digestive system. The table tells you some of the ways you can prevent injury and illness.

Remember, if you think something is wrong with your body, you should always talk to a trained medical professional, like a doctor or a school nurse. Regular medical checkups are an important part of maintaining a healthy body.

Illness or injury	Cause	Symptoms	Prevention	Treatment
Constipation	Too little exercise; stress; lack of fiber in the diet.	Hard **feces** that are difficult to get out.	Include more fiber in the diet; reduce stress; increase exercise.	Take a mild laxative to soften the feces.
Cystitis	Infection by *E. coli* **bacteria**; poor hygiene.	Increasing pain and burning while urinating.	Drink lots of water; eat a healthy diet; good personal hygiene.	Take an **antibiotic** to combat the infection.
Diarrhea	Bacterial or **viral** infection; some toxic substances; nervousness or stress.	Watery feces; uncontrollable urge to rush to use the toilet.	Good hygiene in personal care and food handling.	Drink plenty of water; take antibiotics for a bacterial infection.
Heartburn	Overeating; emotional upset or stress; eating certain "trigger" foods.	Burning sensation in the middle of the chest.	Eat smaller meals; reduce stress; avoid trigger foods.	Take antacid tablets to neutralize the stomach **acid.**

Illness or injury	Cause	Symptoms	Prevention	Treatment
Hemorrhoids	Lack of fiber in the diet; straining to get rid of feces.	Swollen veins in **anal** canal; pain; some bleeding.	Include more fiber in the diet.	Warm baths; sores can be shrunken by drugs, freezing, restricting their blood supply, or surgery.
Indigestion	Overeating; eating too quickly; stress; eating certain "trigger" foods.	Pain after a meal; bloated, sick feeling.	Eat smaller meals; eat more slowly; reduce stress; avoid trigger foods.	Vomiting gets rid of excess or problem food; antacids can help.
Irritable Bowel Syndrome (IBS)	Stress or depression; lack of fiber in the diet.	Diarrhea and constipation, abdominal cramps and pains; loss of appetite; vomiting.	Reduce stress; include more fiber in the diet.	Some drugs can help to control the symptoms.
Tooth decay	Damage to teeth by acid from bacteria in the mouth.	Mild to severe toothache.	Eat a diet rich in calcium; avoid sweets; practice good dental hygiene; have regular dental checkups.	Clean teeth; drill out damaged tooth tissue and replace it with filling; remove tooth in severe cases.

Further Reading

Morrison, Ben. *The Digestive System.* New York: Rosen Publishing Group, Inc., 2000.

Swanson, Diane. *Burp!: The Most Interesting Book You'll Ever Read about Eating.* Buffalo N.Y.: Kids Can Press, 2001.

Toriello, James. *The Stomach: Learning How We Digest.* New York: Rosen Publishing Group, Inc., 2001.

Whelan, Jo. *Diabetes.* Austin, Tex.: Raintree Publishers, 2002.

GLOSSARY

acid liquid that is sour to taste, can eat away metals, and is neutralized by alkalis and bases

alkali substance that has the opposite properties of an acid

amino acid basic unit of a protein molecule

anemia condition involving a lack of hemoglobin in the blood

antibiotic drug used to destroy harmful bacteria and fungi

anus opening through which solid waste leaves the body

artery large blood vessel carrying blood away from the heart

bacterium (plural is **bacteria**) microorganism that can cause infection

bile liquid produced by the liver that helps to break down fats

bolus lump of food that is swallowed

capillary very fine blood vessel that links arteries and veins

carbohydrate nutrient that can be broken down to release energy

chemotherapy treatment of disease, especially cancer, by the use of chemical substances

chyme partly digested liquid food that leaves the stomach

circular muscle muscle arranged in a ring shape

defecation removal of solid waste from the body

diffusion movement of molecules from an area of high concentration to an area of low concentration

digestion process of breaking food down into smaller units

enzyme protein that speeds up chemical reactions

excrete to get rid of waste substances

fat substance that stores and releases energy

fat-soluble able to be dissolved in oils or fats

fatty acid basic unit of a fat molecule

feces solid waste material that leaves the body

food allergy sensitivity to a particular food that may lead to an allergic reaction

gastric having to do with the stomach

glottis space between the vocal cords at the top of the larynx

glucose sugar that stores and releases energy

glycerol substance that combines with fatty acids to make fats

glycogen sugar that can be stored by the body

hemoglobin compound found in red blood cells that transports oxygen around the body

hepatic having to do with the liver

hormone chemical made in the body that travels around the body and affects organs and tissues in a variety of ways

immune system body's natural defense mechanism against infection and disease

insoluble unable to be dissolved

insulin hormone produced by the pancreas

jaundice condition that causes the skin to turn yellowish as excess bile pigments build up in the blood

longitudinal muscle muscle that runs straight up and down

lymphatic system system of drainage vessels that is also involved in the body's immune responses

mineral one of a number of chemicals needed by the body in very small amounts, such as calcium and iron

molecule smallest unit or particle of a substance made of two or more joined atoms

mucosa layer of tissue that produces mucus

mucus sticky, slimy fluid that provides lubrication in the body

nutrient part of our food that the body can use

pancreas abdominal organ that produces insulin and other hormones

peristalsis wavelike motion of muscles that pushes food along the alimentary canal

peritoneum membrane lining the abdominal cavity and covering the organs within it

protein type of large molecule that makes up some of the basic structures of all living things

radiation treatment of disease, especially cancer, by the use of X-rays or similar radiation

renal having to do with the kidneys

saliva digestive juice made by salivary glands in the mouth

sphincter ring of muscle that closes an opening

synthesis process of making something new

valve mechanism for controlling the flow of a liquid through a tube

vein large blood vessel carrying blood back to the heart

virus very small microorganism that can cause infection

vitamin one of a number of complex chemicals that the body needs in very small amounts

water-soluble able to be dissolved in water

INDEX